JONI

The Lyrical Life of Joni Mitchell

JONI

The Lyrical Life of

Joni Mitchell

For my dear sister, Karen,
who shared our turbulent, creative, and often hilarious Canadian childhood.
And a special thanks to Jill Davis, Chelsea C. Donaldson, and Liz Byer for bringing this book to life.

By Selina Alko

HARPER
An Imprint of HarperCollinsPublishers

Joni Mitchell painted with words.

Sitting at her piano or strumming the guitar, she turned the words into songs.

The songs were like brushstrokes on a canvas, saying things that were not only happy or sad but true.

But before the songs, there was a restless girl named Roberta Joan Anderson, who danced in wide-open spaces to the songs of seagulls and the shimmer of her own star.

Young Joni drew pictures of animals, forest fires, and wild flowers. Her mother, Myrtle, took her out to the fields and taught her birdcalls.

There was a lone train, the quiet of nature, and a small town in Canada.

But sometimes Joni felt at odds in the Anderson house, like an upside-down bird on a wire.

It's not that her parents didn't love her, but they were cautious and fixed in their ways.

It seemed to Joni that Myrtle was always cleaning, but one time, she told her daughter: "I'll allow you to paint on the wall of your room."

At piano lessons, Joni made up
her own melodies.

Rainbows tiptoed and jumped
and skipped in her head.

But when Joni was ten years old,
something terrible happened.

She caught a contagious disease called
polio and was taken away to a faraway
hospital with strict rules.

The girl who loved dancing and painting
and music was ordered to lie perfectly still.

Six weeks passed with only one visit from Joni's mother. It was on Christmas that Myrtle brought a small tree to the hospital to cheer her daughter up.

Later that same night, the sounds of carols echoed through empty halls, reminding Joni of home.

Oh, how she wished she could kick and scream. Instead, she shouted the words out loud, her dusky-throated voice cackling, wanting to be heard.

"I will make something of myself,"
she promised the Christmas tree.

And she did.

It began in junior high. The Andersons moved to Saskatoon, where a teacher named Mr. Kratzmann admired Joni's paintings. He encouraged her to look deep inside herself.

He said, "If you can paint with a brush, you can paint with words."

Paintings turned to **poems on the page.**

In high school, Joni was desperate for a guitar to entertain her friends with.

"No!" said her mom, so Joni saved up $36 to buy a ukulele.

Later on, modeling at a local department store earned her enough money to buy her first guitar.

THE FOLKSINGER'S GUITAR GUIDE
PETE SEEGER

But she wanted to do more than just play for her friends. When Joni finally left Saskatoon, it was to go to art school in Calgary, where she found a world of coffeehouses and poetry and a captivating music scene.

Hearing about a folk festival in Toronto, Joni and her boyfriend left school to take a three-day train trip across Canada. In the rhythm of the train's wheels she heard a lonely, bluesy sound and wrote her first song.

Months passed, and even though her boyfriend left for California, Joni stayed on in Toronto, writing music every day. In cafés around town, she sang songs written by other people.

When Joni met an American folk singer named Chuck Mitchell, she thought she had found a partner—he was older and full of fancy words and promises.

Joni packed a guitar case of dreams, moved to Detroit, and changed her name to **Joni Mitchell**.

Everyone loved Joni's voice. But Joni didn't love being married.

There was a thunderstorm of feelings, anger and tears, and performing her own songs for the very first time.

Through it all, Joni kept writing her feelings
down. And the stanzas turned to songs.

Joni saw music everywhere.

On a flight one time, she looked up from her book and noticed the clouds from above and below. How different the clouds looked from both sides. What about looking at her own life that way? There was so much to learn about life, and so much to learn about love, too.

ROWS AND FLOES OF ANGEL HAIR AND ICE CREAM CASTLES IN THE AIR . . . .

Next, Joni followed her music to New York City. Her neighborhood, Chelsea, was abuzz with energy. There were a thousand stories on a single block. The sounds of horns and people and pigeons drifted through butterscotch curtains.

Joni wrote her feelings of joy and wonder into a song called "Chelsea Morning."

A CHELSEA MORNING AND THE FIRST THING THAT I HEARD WAS A SONG OUTSIDE MY WINDOW AND THE TRAFFIC WROTE THE WORDS...

Downtown in Greenwich Village, Joni's music heroes sang folk songs like the ones she was writing—spoken-word stories sung out loud.

When it was Joni's turn to sing, they couldn't believe their ears. Her songs were strong and honest and truly astonishing.

Peace and love and freedom were in the California air.

Joni moved into a groovy house with music and singing and far-out new harmonies.

She was writing song after song about everything around her.

In the summer of '69, all of Joni's friends were going to Woodstock, a music festival in upstate New York.

Joni wanted to go and perform, but she worried she wouldn't make it back in time to go on TV the next day.

BY THE TIME WE GOT TO WOODSTOCK...

STOP THE WAR NOW! PEACE

3 DAYS PEACE MUSIC

Yasgur's Farm

WOODSTOCK NY

HALF MILLION

When she saw what she had missed—singing and guitars and campfires, and sunshine that bloomed into rain showers—she painted her left-out feelings into the song "Woodstock."

When Joni performed "Woodstock," it brought back the intensity of missing the experience. She sang, "We've got to get ourselves back to the garden."

Hearing it, her fans felt like they were part of something bigger than themselves. They felt like she was right there sitting next to them, singing songs about sadness and beauty and hope.

Hearing all these natural feelings sung out loud helped people feel understood.

But outside of the garden, Joni saw humans destroying nature with buildings and cars.

She was so upset that she painted her feelings into a snappy song called "Big Yellow Taxi."

THEY PAVED.

PARADISE... AND PUT UP A PARKING LOT...

SUGAR
MOUNTAIN

...the seasons...

...go round and round and round again...

When her friend Neil Young wrote a song about wanting to stay young forever, she answered playfully with a tune of her own called "The Circle Game."

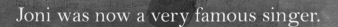

Joni was now a very famous singer.

She traveled to Europe and camped
out on an island in Greece.

She fell in and out of love and
she cried all the time.

She dreamed she was a plastic bag and that people could see right through her.

She took her feelings of love and anger and jealousy and painted a string of songs into an album called *Blue*.

By the time Joni was thirty-five, she moved away from folk music, experimenting with new sounds. Rock and pop and then jazz.

She met a great musician named Charles Mingus, who shared her spirit of honesty. Joni put her voice and her words to his music, and made an album called *Mingus.*

There were dozens of different guitar tunings, a synthesizer, and electric new vibes.

Maybe her fans didn't like it as much as her earlier music, but Joni didn't care.

SONG TO
A SEAGULL
1968

CLOUDS
1969

LADIES OF
THE CANYON
1970

WILD THINGS
RUN FAST
1982

CHALK MARK
IN A RAIN STORM
1988

DON JUAN'S
RECKLESS
DAUGHTER
1977

MINGUS
1979

DOG
EAT DOG
1985

NIGHT
RIDE HOM
1991

"I sing my sorrow, and I paint
my joy," Joni once said.

BLUE
1971

FOR THE ROSES
1972

COURT AND SPARK
1974

HISSING OF SUMMER LAWNS
1975

HEJIRA
1976

TURBULENT INDIGO
1994

TAMING THE TIGER
1998

BOTH SIDES NOW
2000

TRAVELOGUE
2002

SHINE
2007

Her songs show us the way by telling us her truth.

Truth gives us freedom. And freedom gives us *wings to fly.*

Author's Note

I was nine years old when I first listened to Joni Mitchell's songs, at sleepaway camp on an island in British Columbia, Canada.

I strung bracelets with my friends to Joni's songs "The Circle Game" and "Big Yellow Taxi." During the school year, whenever I heard these songs, camp memories would rush back, making me feel warm and happy—reassuring me that I'd be back at camp again when the next season came around.

In this book I attempt to capture some of the many creative influences throughout Joni's life. As a little girl in Canada she relished the quiet beauty of nature, she drew and painted, and she kept scrapbooks of wild flowers. And later, as a young woman, she was thrilled by the vibrant sounds on the streets of Chelsea, New York ("I heard . . . a song outside my window, and the traffic wrote the words"). Her many love relationships—with Graham Nash, Leonard Cohen, James Taylor, David Crosby, Sam Shepard, and others—were formative to her songwriting, too.

She began with drawing and painting as her driving passions, and then she applied her intuitive artistic principles to her songwriting. Just as some artists exaggerate colors to convey emotion, Joni has done the same with her brutally honest, vividly poetic lyrics. While she is a successful musician, she remains a visual artist, creating the artwork on many of her album covers, including "Ladies of the Canyon," "Song to a Seagull," "Clouds," "Both Sides Now," and "Turbulent Indigo."

In creating Joni's story for this picture book, I felt as if I was on a personal journey of self-discovery, remembering my earliest creative and artistic influences—a captive on my own "carousel of time." When I was midway through these paintings, my own kids began going to the same camp where I first heard Joni Mitchell—and when I saw pictures of them there, it brought me right back to the island in British Columbia where my happiest memories live.

Selina Alko

Discography

Song to a Seagull. 1968. Reprise.

Clouds. 1969. Reprise.

Ladies of the Canyon. 1970. Reprise.

Blue. 1971. Reprise.

For the Roses. 1972. Elektra/Asylum.

Court and Spark. 1974. Elektra/Asylum.

Miles of Aisles. 1974. Elektra/Asylum.

The Hissing of Summer Lawns. 1975. Elektra/Asylum.

Hejira. 1976. Elektra/Asylum.

Don Juan's Reckless Daughter. 1977. Elektra/Asylum.

Mingus. 1979. Elektra/Asylum.

Shadows and Light. 1980. Elektra/Asylum.

Wild Things Run Fast. 1982. Geffen.

Dog Eat Dog. 1985. Geffen.

Chalk Mark in a Rain Storm. 1988. Geffen.

Night Ride Home. 1991. Geffen.

Turbulent Indigo. 1994. Reprise.

Hits. 1996. Reprise.

Misses. 1996. Reprise.

Taming the Tiger. 1998. Reprise.

Both Sides Now. 2000. Reprise.

Travelogue. 2002. Nonesuch.

Shine. 2007. Hear Music.

Bibliography

Evans, Mike and Paul Kingsbury, eds. *Woodstock: Three Days That Rocked the World.* New York: Sterling Publishing, 2009.

Fleischer, Leonore. *Joni Mitchell.* New York: Flash Books, 1976.

Jonimitchell.com. Official website.

Marom, Malka. *Joni Mitchell: In Her Own Words.* Toronto: ECW Press, 2014.

Myers, Marc. *Anatomy of a Song: The Oral History of 45 Iconic Hits That Changed Rock, R&B and Pop.* New York: Grove Press, 2016.

Paglia, Camille. *Break, Blow, Burn: Camille Paglia Reads Forty-Three of the World's Best Poems.* New York: Pantheon Books, 2005.

Smith, Zadie. "Some Notes on Attunement: A Voyage around Joni Mitchell." *New Yorker,* December 17, 2012.

Weller, Sheila. *Girls Like Us: Carole King, Joni Mitchell, Carly Simon—and the Journey of a Generation.* New York: Simon & Schuster, 2008.

Yaffe, David. *Reckless Daughter: A Portrait of Joni Mitchell.* New York: Farrar, Straus and Giroux, 2017.